Beneath the Blue Umbrella

poems by

Karen Marker

Finishing Line Press
Georgetown, Kentucky

Beneath the Blue Umbrella

Dedicated to

Susan Cosens 1944–2023
&
Eva Marker 1917–2005

who paved my path with poetry

ACKNOWLEDGMENTS

There are countless people I owe thanks to for the birth of this book. This includes
the many poets in my writing communities who have inspired me with their work,
and encouraged me to keep going, especially those who came before me with their
published FLP chapbooks: Louise Moises, Susan Vespoli, Sandra Anfang,
Yiskah Rosenfeld and Angie Minkin. I would also not have been able to write any
of these poems without the support of my teachers and mentors, Genine Lentine,
Kathleen McClung, Stewart Florsheim, Jannie Dresser, Diane Frank, Hollie Hardy,
Francesca Bell, George Doyle and Jerry Hickerson. Finally I would not have the
courage to have started down the path and the stamina to continue without the
unceasing support of my husband and first reader Andy Wolpert, and my children
Rachel and Sophie Lee.

Thanks to the editors and publications that gave first homes to these poems:
"I've been Following You on Instagram"—*The MacGuffin*
"In April"—*The Benicia Literary Review*

Profits from Beneath the Blue Umbrella will be donated to NAMI (National
Association of Mental Illness.)

Publisher: Leah Huete de Maines
Editor: Christen Kincaid
Cover Art: "Germination" by Jules Roman
Author Photo: Michael Richardson
Cover Design: Elizabeth Maines McCleavy

Order online: www.finishinglinepress.com
also available on amazon.com

Author inquiries and mail orders:
Finishing Line Press
PO Box 1626
Georgetown, Kentucky 40324
USA

Contents

The Body of My Work

I always wanted to be somewhere else
so I'd hang myself like clothes
in a closet, right-handed
hold on to a pen
as tight as I could
in the dark
I'd get naked with paper
ask myself
what does ugly look like
where does beautiful begin
this story I started over
so many times
I now have an arthritic thumb
calloused fingers, my knees
can't crouch in the corners
I can hardly make it up
the stairs, but every day's scratch
has made me better
at finding my way
back to that beginning
when I was the child
in a dance class
spinning over the floor—
almost flying—
wearing a red velvet dress

Under the Full Flower Moon

The month begins with falling
petals like tears cherry trees shed,

dark clouds covering a hole
of light. The sky makes

a hollow ring around roses
just opened. You can't see

where the music comes from—
only your heart can hear

the crush of ashes beneath
the blue umbrella.

Today Like Every Other Day
—after Rilke

I wake up missing you and you are right there
making coffee in the kitchen
outside the window
the little birds are busy drinking rainwater
from camellia buds, a thousand jasmine flowers
are about to open, the wisteria blooms
today I wake up forgetting
it is not you in the kitchen
you have been gone
almost twenty years
Really? No! I must count again
I forget what year it is
how old my children are
where I left my keys, my wallet,
how to drive a car
I forget how it started
this being frightened of driving
when that's all I once wanted
to drive out into this world
as far away as I could get
from Ohio and from you
with your sad eyes, your long letters
once or twice a week you wrote
these faded letters, the only thing I kept
not one of them thrown away
or lost even when I had nowhere
permanent to stay
thousands of letters ripe as buds
bundled up in boxes
and today, like every other day
the boxes of letters are still in my study
and I don't take them out, open them, start reading
there are more letters too, from my sister
because writing letters was what we did
and I've saved them all
so maybe I could go back one day
and remember what we didn't have
but today is not the day
when she's almost as old as you were
when you died, or at least became dead

to who you'd been—dementia dead
and she's dead too to who she once was
I don't want to remember her like this
in between living and dying
when she's forgotten she once was a poet
who could play Mozart Sonatas
today I don't want to pick up the phone
try to get a nurse to take it to her
in her room where she tells me
about a party she's going to later
today like every day I've woken up empty
startled to hear your voice
telling me to be kind to my sister because
she couldn't be anyone else, you say
don't be frightened because you still have music
how could I forget how important that was
you would play first, after, play away
the loss, find your comfort
so today I too start this way, with the ground
my feet cold, wet, muddy
I don't look at the dirty dishes
from last night's dinner
don't wash the kitchen floor
climb up to clean the cobwebs
from the mirror, but today
like every other day I get married again
and again and again to the bird outside
to the promise of peace I can't keep
I don't think of the break, the next foot fall
who will hold my hand, keep me walking
who will care for the house
where the money will come from
if there's a run on the bank, who will die
today I say I do I do I do
make it one long continuous breath

The Last Goodbye to My House on Hill Street

I don't remember when I first noticed it. It was just a little splash of paint on the unfinished boards of the wood steps leading upstairs but at various times I thought of it as a galloping horse, a silver slipper, a piece of cloud. Most often I thought of it as a magic key that only I knew was there, that could open a secret door into another world.

At some point it had become my custom to go every day to check on it, to be sure it was still there. On my way I'd pass by the avocado tree that had grown tall in the alcove. As I looked at the silver spot I'd think about how that tree had sprouted from the pit that my mother had first placed in a cup by the kitchen window. I was always surprised how it had grown faster than I had, and through all that time the silver mark had stayed the same size.

Our Techbuilt house was the only house I'd known. It had been delivered on a truck and assembled on a cement slab at the top of a hill on the edge of a forest in Hamden. For most of the time we lived there, the upstairs had remained unfinished. It had only one big room with glass windows and plywood floors. On rainy days my mother would pack up a picnic and pretend she was taking my little sister and me on a hike into the Rocky Mountains that she was always missing. Sometimes we would dress up in the clothes that Aunt Reba had sent us from her store in San Francisco. The fur coats, satin slips, high heeled shoes and stockings that we pulled out of a cardboard box became costumes for our plays. If the well and the septic system stopped working, the toilet overflowed and we had to gather water in buckets, which really made it feel like we were camping.

When I was five a new room was finally made upstairs. Our big sister's bedroom was the only room in our house that had real polished hardwood floors and me and my little sister weren't allowed to go in there without her permission. She didn't have to worry anymore that we would be in the room next to hers, where we could put our ears up to the folding accordion wall and hear everything she said to her boyfriend, even when they were whispering. But right after it became her bedroom, when she was sweet sixteen, and had a beautiful dress in the closet she was going to wear to the prom, something bad happened. Our sister was gone. When we saw her again she looked like her room without her in it. Our parents said the hospital was going to make her better, she'd be coming back, and her room was still private. For two years I waited for her and all that time the silver spot going up the stairs was still there. Now I had just finished second grade and I had gone inside the house one last time to say goodbye because we were moving to Ohio.

Our best friends, the family who lived in the Techbuilt house next to ours, Kiki, Teeter, Robby, Skipper and their mom Dottie, were standing at the edge of our driveway. The moving truck had already gone with the boxes. Our suitcases were packed, the house was empty, and we were ready to head off down Hill Street. My father was calling for me to come out. I had just enough time to bend down to kiss the spot on the stairs goodbye. My big sister wasn't coming with us. She was not there with the neighbors waving and crying. I knew I would never see that spot again. And no one else would ever know it was there.

Even if No One Taught You How

Grief grabs you with a gut punch,
a warning scream like fighter jets
close overhead, the wail
of boats moving down river,
a train's shrill whistle
and roar letting you know
it's not stopping—
she's not coming back.

Quick! Cover the mirrors.
Sit low to the ground.
A leg of the chair has broken,
your shirt is torn
right down the middle.
No time to fix it.
Dig a hole, throw the dirt
before the ghosts take over
the mounds of garbage,
discarded beer cans,
cardboard shelters.
Before your teeth take hold
like a dog, her death
in your mouth.

Say her name,
and again, say it with praise
for the beauty
as you bury her—
name it everlasting.

The Day My Sister Died

The green grows heavy
in New Orleans,
we can feel its weight.
Mules bray all night.
They can feel the storm coming.
Wind sweeps through the rooms
of our shotgun house,
leaves behind a trail of litter.
More rain, more green pops out.

A lone black-eyed Susan
drops yellow petals
on the side of the path.

Upriver in Minneapolis
my sister died.
How could the water
move down here so fast,
and for a moment flow back
before it got to the sea?

It wasn't meant to be like this.
She should be picking out plants
at the nursery, growing hostas,
bleeding hearts, wood leeks.
She should be smelling the purple lilacs
in Lyndale Park,
watching the weeping cherry,
the arch of roses,
walking the lakes
named after women.

Instead she's in the bardo,
dirt under her nails,
and I'm booking a flight.

Soon there will be no more crossing.
Even at the minus tide the space
from bank to bank has grown
too wide.

Dance of the Three Sisters

We hold her like an empty bowl
in the company of a tribe of dancers.
Dedicate the class to releasing her spirit.
Name her so we can feel her fly
into our arms, our legs. Like Minnehaha Falls,
like water streaming over wings.

Minneapolis, city of lakes and butterflies.
Early summer light beams
through the studio windows.

Dance filled the place of worship
in our sister's life so it's the best we can do:
we two younger sisters make this memorial
on a smooth wooden floor surrounded by mirrors
reflecting ourselves back to each other.

The teacher instructs us in three improvisations.
We start with *Agitation*. Know all too well
the trembling she did. A whirlwind need
to elevate left her wanting more.
She practiced for hours.

Dance flowed through her fingers
when she played piano.
It fed her poetry. Her mantra—
never stop moving.

Lose Control comes next. How hard
she'd tried not to feel the fury
of her losses, a shock to watch
her face freeze in that space
she'd kept deeply hidden.

Embody Impact—after the pieces
are broken, bitter, bent
but still related—
we prance across the floor,
come back together.
Our sister, here and not here.

Into the Mystery of Mental Illness

On Memorial Day at Lakewood Cemetery
we don't talk about the terror or our grief
for what's missing as we wander this city of tombstones
amidst flowers and flags left on soldiers' graves.

Everyone's gone who would remember
the man who had been our sister's father
and she's just joined our mother
who'd said too much but never enough
about what had happened.

The cover of the niche with her cremains
is now closed forever. Her father's grave I found
on Google—a military cemetery in Denver,
his stone with these words engraved:
Captain, Medical Corp, World War II.

His daughter was conceived before he left
but it wasn't the war that killed him. Keith's name
lived on like a knife, an unsheathed sword,
a shadow caught in our throats. A psychiatrist,
he walked into our dreams, sat at the foot
of our sister's bed, haunting with words unsaid.

What terrible things had he seen in the minds
of wounded men, the traumas he treated?
He'd chosen to admit himself to Menninger's,
so few options for treating his illness
and still he'd traveled as a ghost
of kept secrets, a shiver.

I found him in the 1950 census with our mother.
Our sister, age six. How long did that last,
the wish for a different life, before he told them
they had to start over without him? And why
all those years later, right before our sister married,
had he signed out for the day, gone to a park,
shot himself in the head?

There's no crack in the locked door
we can listen through for answers.

Schizophrenic

We shiver when we say it:
like we've been bit—
schizophrenia,
a snake bite, needle prick
poison, blood drops
with that diagnosis,
a split: life/death.

There should have been family therapy,
my younger sister says.
That could have saved us
from what happened next—
the label, a word
wrongly used on her.
The consequences kept coming
and now she can't undo
the damage the pills did
to her kidneys.

Our older sister from a different father
couldn't get back her memories
after electric shock.
At sixteen they called her catatonic.
She sat immobile in a stupor
and then we all wandered
in catacombs filled with water,
slowly drowning.

Everyone was contaminated—
the shame of this sentence
from our sister's father,
all we couldn't say that doubled.
The doctors thought it better
his daughter didn't get too close
to his dislodged brain
but the genes of his trauma
were already in the pool
of our mother's body.
I can't unhold how it happened.

Menninger's Sanitorium

"Hope is an adventure, a going forward, a confident
search for a rewarding life."
    Dr. Karl Menninger

It's the first capital of the world for mental illness treatment,
gem of the city beside the river, so close to the pastoral
green ash, oak, dogwood, American sycamore, native prairie grass.

Pictures show it's almost gutted, seen from all directions
on Martin's Hill, all that's left—abandoned ruins,
boarded up windows, ghosts of former residents
who pace the halls of landmark limestone buildings
with a replica of Independence Hall,
the tower's clock with frozen hands.

Her hands froze when she made the ride in the 40's
to Topeka from Denver. A long drive in the winter.
Many times she'd almost skidded off the road
so she could sit beside her husband Keith.
She'd known him as a trombone player, whistler, dancer,
who loved chewing juicyfruit gum.
They met in high school, their lives
always a beautiful adventure.
His psychiatry board exam scores were perfect.

Behind these walls everyone had a part to play.
Because everything else had failed,
they worked together. A doctor first,
a colleague, Keith was a treasured patient,
not just a vet from the war in need of better therapy.
Dr. Menninger was his mentor—his book *The Human Mind*
turned psychiatry into a science—they may have been friends
before their lives took such a different course.

He'd told his wife she should stop coming back.
Her love wasn't going to cure him.
Years later his confidential records were shredded.
A video advertises the property. How important
to find a buyer who will preserve it.

Rorschach Questions

1.
The cards were in the basement
along with everything else she'd been holding onto—
drawings, poster paint, construction paper
we'd folded to make mirror images of elephants.
How was it my mother still had them,
his name carefully written
on the corner of the musty gray pack next to the name
Hermann Rorschach Psychodiagnostic Plates?
The very cards he'd used in his studies
of psychopathic World War II soldiers
for *The American Journal of Psychiatry*
before people talked of post-traumatic stress.

All the things my mother failed
to mention—I can't remember
if I'd asked her why they were there.
She must have carried them cross country,
so many years of transport house to house
then kept them in a corner that flooded
before she handed them over that day
like a present.

There I was following her schizophrenic
first husband's footsteps. I'd kept quiet
about my studies until that moment.
Would she curse my choice of profession,
fear I'd too lose my mind, or maybe find something
more forbidden about dark parts of her past?

2.
When they became mine to use and interpret
I touched and turned each one he'd touched.
Asked myself *what did he see when he looked at card A?*
Bat? Butterfly? Dark ghost of a father?
When he looked at the shape of the ink's black
blurring into another did it speak to him
of what was falling apart, the brain's disintegration,
the force that dropped his family into division—
or what might happen if he started over?

3.
Such crazy kindling kin make.
Nothing makes sense
when the white boards are wiped clean.
We heard how much it hurt,
but now we need a different diagnosis
from the one he'd been given.
Rorschach/tarot/tea leaves—we can always see
a double, another father, mother, mirror image,
blank walls reflecting back questions: who will fall in
to looking like Narcissus? who is fairest?
who will eat the poisoned apple? who can I call?
why didn't I ask my mother
the date she first married,
how Keith's cards got into my hands,
can we ever really be healed from trauma?
All I know is my work with the cards,
looking for answers, leads to a blue gray line
where the sea meets the sky
and stays there, silent.

Obituary

They clouded her, crowded her out,
pulled her under. She was heavy
with them passing into and over her
grandmother, grandfather, uncle, father

crossed eyes, hooked nose, the shadows
that were her father's German father's face,
crooked brain paths, itching hives,
contagion we can no longer see
pulled her under

her only memory of her father
that day he took her hand
his wire rim glasses glinting
as he lifted her up and over the sidewalk

when she had thought she could fly
how much farther she fell, no hand
to hold when she could not walk
how quickly she drowned—

only a hooded figure to follow,
no rope to pull her back

no one ever told her she had surviving family
who knew how to pronounce
the first surname she'd been given
and tell her there might be
a different ending.

Battle Baby
for Bill

You were baptized in battles—
a German grandfather's blood,
one of the *babies* sent to the Bulge
to prevent Hitler's last crossing.
Criss-crossing, tightening, loosening,
lost, you were dropped down
to clean up the mess.
Whatever was golden
already had curdled.

Still a boy you went missing in action,
carried by the feet
your podiatrist father
had taught you how to preserve.
The skills you'd learned
from the mountains,
kept you alive
when you wandered the forest
among shredded corpses only to come home
to your beloved brother's
shredding brain.

All of this was in the head you shot,
that opened like a book
into your mother's losses.
Those who'd died too soon.
You had to go before your older brother did,
even if it meant you'd leave your son, age ten—

the same age you'd been that day
you pulled your father back
on a sled in the snow
after his heart had stopped
and you couldn't save him.

The Artist's Song

        nightingale's voice
        soars over gravestones
        fills the dark

The children huddled under the bed when their father's drunken rages started. Bill had a brilliant mind when we married but the trembling in his hands had only grown worse. I don't remember the fight that triggered him to shoot himself at thirty-five. After all the hurts I learned to forgive and start over, to know the difference between what I could change and what I couldn't. You can play with the clay, not the casting in bronze. Most of all I owe my survival to art. There's a park full of my sculptures on the river where I've returned to my roots. At ninety-five I have so much gratitude for the earth and sky. My new great grandchild. This beautiful life. My paintings that I see as prayers. I paint my rooms green, draw the begonia by my open window, make its underbelly translucent red. The leaves reach out towards the light, the wind stirs the curtains. The curtains are clear enough to see through to the trees.

        skins shed
        a snake grows
        another life

Serenity Prayer for Nana

You were left like a sea urchin
at the minus tide on an emptied shore.
What courage you needed to stay alive.

Just two when your father died, five
when you lost your older brother.
Then you lost your husband Doc,
your two sons. To calm yourself
you kept the serenity prayer
by your bed with a vase of flowers.
God's gifts, you said.

You closed your curtains,
covered your sofas with plastic,
put lace doilies on the corners.
Your china dolls sat there
with their blue eyes unblinking.

Little Susan called you Nana,
said you made her frightened,
how you scratched your eczema.
Later she had hives
when she thought of having children.
The itching stopped when her tubes were tied.

You willed her the proceeds
from the family farm. She bought herself a house,
filled it with flowers and calm.

Susan, we thought, was the end of your line.
She'd given up on God and didn't fear dying.
But on tiny fragments of paper,
in your loopy cursive, we found you'd written
other names, two more grandchildren
who called you Nana. One had a child.

The tides come back
with a sigh like a prayer
while the moon pulls this story
it's my job to tell.

Resume: My Education

1. First Lessons from Bear Path School Elementary and the Yale Psychiatric Institute

My kindergarten classmates, their parents, my teacher asked *what happened to your sister?* Carefully I repeated the words I'd been told to say: *she's in the hospital because she has a mental illness.* Everyone went silent so I stopped talking about that morning she went missing, days before Christmas, or about how scared I felt when my parents left every Wednesday night for a meeting and how sometimes I'd go to a brick building where I waited on a metal chair in the lobby, and when my sister came out she looked like a ghost. I was six. At school we had nap time, played with toys in a sandbox, learned to write our alphabet.

2. Recording My Feelings

Our father bought a reel-to-reel tape recorder. It seemed like magic, how the gray tape circled around, and later we could hear our voices. He set up a microphone and my little sister and I went upstairs to his small office in the back corner of the house. Most of the time we talked about how much we missed our sister. How she had a boyfriend named Bob who loved baked beans and she let us follow them around. We hoped she'd be coming home soon. Sometimes while the tape was going we'd scream and hurt each other by hurling stones. Later we lost that tape we had listened to over and over. All I had left were the voices in my head, what I thought I had said.

3. Being Studied at the Gesell Institute

My parents made me a dollhouse out of wooden crates with cut out windows and doors. They filled it with little wooden chairs, tables, beds, chests of drawers. There were four doll children in the family, and everyone had a room of their own. I loved to play with my doll family for hours every day, but it was strange when I was taken to an office where there was a doll house and a doctor who watched me while I played. I couldn't understand why he asked me questions like *what is the father doing? where is the mother? What happens in the bedroom?*

4. What I Found in the Attic

I could get into the attic by climbing up a ladder in the hallway of the Honeywell's house we'd bought in Ohio. That's where I'd cracked the lock on my sister's diary from the year I turned one and found out it had been the best year of her life. She had so many crushes who came to her twelfth birthday party where they did square dancing. And she'd loved having me as her baby sister. So why when she left the hospital had she gone to live with the Schwartz's in New Haven instead of coming home to live with us? The year I turned twelve, after she asked me to be in her wedding, I found a big trunk filled with letters, medical school records, a photograph of a strange man dressed as a captain, holding my mother's hand. That's when I heard my mother take the call in the kitchen, when I saw her cry, when she told me he had been my sister's father, and now he was dead.

The Cube and Free Fall

you constructed a cube
a prison house, a prism
perfect life

three-dimensional, geometric sphere
perfection the whole
of your world's weight

you could never see all sides
at once, your final stage
immobility, the truth
you'd lost—

nothing will hold you
together and last forever

the counterpart of a sphere—
a fishing hole, dark eyes
exposed far beneath
the surface, silver in black
water when something
leaps in the shadows

you must be ready
for the puncture made
in ice
where you could fall through
between melting and freezing
here and gone

in the deep pool
you can see yourself reflected,
a thousand seeds of sun,
a split pomegranate,
stars spilling out of space
bottomless—
you are always being pulled
into light

I've Been Following You on Instagram

Leonora Carrington, your eerie
paintings with mirrors,
your pet hyena, keep popping
up on my feed, fueling my hunger
for a new year of writing.
Maybe you're laughing right now
while outside it's raining,
surrealistic strokes down the glass,
fallen branches as I watch
how you pictured yourself
on a blue chair, a red cushion
tangled hair, wild wolf-self
newly given birth,
both of you gazing towards me.
In the distance the galloping
horse goes off to the forest.
Maybe you're laughing as I listen
to the story you wrote
about your beast surrogate
who went to the ball,
the bat that flew out the window,
about your mother
who never understood.
Did that lead to what came
later when they carried
you off, locked you up,
thought you'd lost your mind?
The price of your art was more
than the brief cry you made
when you dared to run away
with your love. Often these days
I wake from dreams, fall asleep
forgetting. I'm always missing
my mother who every day
would escape from the world
by finding her way into clouds
that were mountains.
Just like you she was eighteen
that year you wrote your story.
She never went into a mental

hospital but two of her daughters
and her first husband did.
Later she flowered, lost all
her memories, found just the right
wild company to keep.
I'm listening to you both
telling the story, swooshing
in the wind, tearing things down,
saying something else could happen.

In April

When we watched the brides take their time
circling round each other while the red-haired
woman rabbi chanted seven blessings and the brass
band played we knew everyone has a chance at joy.

Because April in New Orleans has the best weather
weddings happen every day. There's so much to love
in this city. It felt like only yesterday we heard the train's
whistle, the whirl of the plane, the long slow call of the boat
down along the curve of the river and took off
in the direction of music that's always somewhere
just around the corner.

Even more festivals are coming interspersed
with miracles. The rising from the dead. The escaping
to freedom through a parting sea. Here we are rising up
like the cypress trees making new trees from knobs
in the grass under the long arms of the oaks, finding brown
speckled eggs fit perfectly into the palm of our hands.

Still we remember even in April disasters happen—
a volcanic eruption, a fire, a flood, an accident, everything
can be lost in a second. Or we may be saved
like the young woman by a bag of kumquats
picked earlier in the day from her father's tree,
strapped to her back, so when a drunken driver
slams into her bike they squish into the shape of her body.
A year later she's alive with a baby. And today
I'm starting where I am, from the beginning.

To Marriage After Divorce: A Villanelle

Marriage you carry so much in your arms.
I've lived it all, both now and long ago
have found your joy and how you may do harm

when signs are missed that something might be wrong.
The first time I had nowhere else to go
when you came to carry me, kept me armed

against raging fires, floods, amidst alarms.
I clung to you, sometimes just to show
my joy could not be broken by the harm

of growing battles. Wanting to belong
I brought in children, so you must have known
how much you carried, tender lives, unarmed

against what happened as we went along.
Nothing prepared them for the final blow,
that fall from joy to ward off further harm,

give second chances. My daughter wasn't charmed,
said no to you but aged to find you'd grown.
Marriage, please carry her more gently in your arms.
Today she claims her joy, vows to do no harm.

First Snowfall

This poem has woven in several words from James Joyce's Ulysses

Let this day be a magic act
  borrowed and born from the folds
of morning—a handkerchief
  shaken and there pop the wings
of a smoke blue bird, the wind in a tree
  with lit up candles singing
happy birthday and *rum tum tum*
  tiddly dum to the center
of the unspoken world issuing breath
  let it be a day we find polliwogs
in the lake, watch them grow up
  my sister and me and our cat
leaping over the edge to *rub-a-dub-dub*
  three maids in a tub—newly speeched
creation—let this be my childhood
  film clips spliced together
let my mobile eyes follow as the moon
  pours milk from the sleeve of the sky
under my flared dress
  my petticoats dance, in black slippers
let me plié on polished wood floors
  look at myself in multiple mirrors
while Ms Stodel waits
  my mother's hands on the keys
of another piano concerto
  let me see the fable of my family
infused with desire, remember
  the first time the screen came down
the lights went up, the first snowfall
  that stayed on the ground
let me recreate wonder
  my parents transparent, hardly touching,
let me go back.

Chasing Butterflies

In Connecticut our back yard that runs out into the forest is all I know about the size of the world. This is where my mother takes us on long summer days after she laces up her hiking boots and packs a picnic lunch. We set off with our butterfly net, splashing along the banks of the stream on our way past the hermit's hut that's surrounded by big dark trees. What I want most is to get to the secret clearing with the soft green moss and the tiny waterfall. As we walk my mother names every flower on the path. She tells us what her father Bo taught her about them and shows us the one she likes best, the jack in the pulpit. She says it reminds her of him because of its quiet bowed head.

This happened before I'd been back to where my mother's life began. I had not yet felt the lightness of the air up high or seen those bright blue days in Denver where the mountains hover overhead. I had not touched the hardness and warmth of the granite stones, gathered the purple lupine and columbine as I followed the path of swallowtails around the lake. Nor had I been to visit my grandfather's Sweden, his farm at Fillinge surrounded by yellow rapeseed fields where at dusk I catch sight of a moose grazing. I had not yet found the trail through pine trees, seen how the summer light lingers all the way until midnight, touched his collection of butterflies kept pressed behind glass.

When we finally reach the clearing I am in my favorite place in the world. I rub my hands across the moss and it feels like my velvet dress which I love so much that when I wear it I don't want to take it off because it makes me feel like dancing. I want to live here forever in this green velvet kingdom and imagine the twelve dancing princesses from the fairy tale and my mother when long ago she was called Little Evie and her father would take her to a cabin in the mountains where he would catch butterflies and she would wander off so long no one would know where she went.

Now we are laying out our lunch on the circle of moss and I am wondering about everything that is hiding in the woods around us. Sometimes I have seen frogs and snakes slither under the leaves on their way to the water. I know there are other creatures that live here too that might come out if I don't look directly at them and just hush like my mother tells me to do. I am certain that fairies, those very little people, live here and they love dancing when I am not watching.

My mother has also told me the story of the *Poor Babes in the Wood*. I'm looking at her now with her strong brown legs, wearing shorts, her long hair pulled into a braid, not like anyone else's mother. I don't yet know that she will never get back to see her father's farm in Sweden. That she didn't even get to say goodbye before Bo died in the sanatorium. And that Bo never went back to see his mother and father, sisters and brothers. I'm hoping my mother won't turn into a deer or a fairy and run off into the woods or back to Denver and leave my little sister and me here in the forest to fend for ourselves and find our way home.

Calling You Back from the Great Beyond

I must go alone up the mountain
where I left you, scattered ash to wind.
Of course you would have stayed there
lodging yourself into bits of granite,
clinging to the edge above the tree line
in the shape of wild lupine, Indian paintbrush
at the Continental Divide, part of you
looking east, part to the west.

For this solitary seance
I will bow to all directions,
spread my fingers wide as if I'm seeking
the keys of a piano. Then with eyes shut,
head up, I will call you like a coyote,
howl for you to hear me.

Mother hear me, I'm your baby, hungry.
I'm your teen, howling, trapped.
I'm a single mother tossed divorce
then death, more death, I've become
an elder, so many of our family gone.

You never showed me how
to grieve so I will scream your name
until it echoes peak to peak
before the full moon rises silent
I will listen hard to what comes back.

When I'm done with howling
I will carry stones in my pockets.
Stack them up, rock cairns, little towers.
I will watch and wait
until they do not tumble
as I ask for you to come.
Again and again and again
I will ask for you to come
and tell me what happened
that hurt you, that you made the choices
not to talk, that you locked up your stories,
left no key, never went back.

I will close my eyes and wait
to catch your whispered answers
to why and why and why again.
Please tell me, teach me,
help me understand
the timeline of your losses
so I won't forget.
That we may heal
I am here to write it out.

Red Fox

The night when you come
like spring's first breath
to my back door I am speechless.

Our eyes lock. For seconds
time stops. What do I call you?

The full pink moon reflects upon
your silver fur as you search for
what I hide inside.

When you turn away you wave
a wide flag tail. I remember the world
I'd lost. The word that is your name.

Tomorrow I will follow your soft foot steps
through the green hills above the city. California
poppies will burst diaphanous among bright
yellow mustard. Coral bells, purple iris,

a baby snake just hatched will appear
on the path with everything else that hungers,
full of hope, still wild and unnamed.

I Need Help with Directions

because there's a crease
where the map's been folded,
because the lines of the streets
are thin and yellowed,
all the names have disappeared,
the borders are blurred.
Maybe it's better I use a compass,
follow stars, take a path
along musical octaves,
or on strings that vibrate.
Maybe I need to find
the halfway point
between burning and freezing,
dark and light, or go sleepwalking
with my voice in repose,
my green bed full of bunting
spinning out the directions
like a dervish dance.
Or maybe my map is a poem
that sings as supplication
to the dead. Because the truth is
I search for graves and won't know
how to get where I'm going
until I've heard someone on the other side
trying to find me, calling my name.

The Forest Preserve
After W.S. Merwin's For the Anniversary of My Death

Every day without knowing it
I have written myself into another forest
I want to preserve.
Entangled in this garment
of green undergrowth, overgrowth,
growth so deep and dark
I cannot find a way through
without a path, I have no choice
but to go further in, to follow
the sound of all that hides,
all that wants to be discovered.

The song of one persistent bird
guides me through my past
to all my future
journeys that won't begin
until I'm thoroughly lost,
until I bow to what is
and to what is not yet.
Climb a tree. Find a clearing
where everything I love is buried.

There's no way to go back
now I've made this forest
the work of my every waking hour.

Karen Marker lives in Oakland, California where she trained and worked as a school psychologist for thirty-five years before retiring at the start of the pandemic and turning her full attention to writing poetry, essays and memoir. In addition to her studies in psychology Karen's formal education includes the Greek classics, drama and the creative process. She also directed a children's theater and wrote and produced plays based on Greek mythology that incorporated the use of puppetry, dance and music. Karen's writing is inspired by family roots and branches in places such as New England, Ohio, New Orleans, Colorado, Lithuania and Sweden and has been honored with awards from the Friendswood Library Ekphrastic Poetry Contest, the Soul-Making Keats Literary Competition and the Ina Coolbrith Circle. She has been published in anthologies and journals including *The MacGuffin, The Monterey Poetry Review, The Haight Ashbury Literary Journal, Wingless Dreamer,* and *Slant Poetry* as well as in *Vistas* and *Byways Literary Review,* where she has also served as an editor. Her poetry can be found in the Kent State University May 4th Special Collections and Archives and has been incorporated into the liturgy of Jewish prayer services. Treasuring family above all else Karen proudly led a love-poetry writing workshop as part of her daughter's inclusive lesbian wedding where transgender and disability rights were at the forefront. In all her work Karen has been committed to using storytelling to address social justice issues and to overcome traumas from loss and stigmas attached to mental illness.